For Ally my lovely lit

For my kiddles Jack

This book is dedicated to Jc

how to cook

Aaron Wright was born in Euston London, not the station of course, but at University College Hospital in July 1969.

It was a momentous event that threatened to overshadow the other landmark in History during that month, the moon landing.

His family moved to a small village in Shropshire called Bishop's Castle when he was 8 which came as a bit of a shock to this city street urchin who was now surrounded by beautiful countryside and not a lot to do.

He escaped to the University of Liverpool at 19 and completed a degree in Communication Studies and Psychology, after which he failed to find his dream job in the media.

In desperation he applied for a PGCE and ended up teaching in the North-East of England where he has lived for the past 30 years.

He regularly attends spoken word nights in the North-East and has performed feature sets at Poetry Jam, King Ink, The Stanza, The Cooking Pot, Under The Arches and Never Mind The Ramones.

A multiple Poetry Slam loser, he celebrated reaching the heady heights of the quarter finals of The Great Northern Slam.

He was also one of the sacrificial poets at the Great Northern Slam 'Champion of Champions' Slam.

He ran Owl Writers from the Outer West Library and then Newcastle Central Library, producing a poetry anthology entitled Breaking Bard that marked the 500th anniversary of the death of Shakespeare. No offence Shaky but you've been dead for half a millennium so it's an excuse to celebrate.

He has written poems and stories for the past 48 years and has been published in the Best of Squiffy Gnu anthology inspired by Jo Bell's 52 project as well as I Am Not A Silent Poet, Sharon Larkin's Good Dadhood project, The Fat Damsel and Writers For Calais.

He is currently attempting to write a thousand poems from the beginning of May 2023 to the end of April 2024. He has created 742 so far and is wondering if quantity is winning over quality.

He has also written several novels and a shedload of short stories and hopes that this book of poems will entertain you and distract you from the everyday pointless of existence.

Dr. Erasmus Croc (his full name is Dr. Erasmus Hieronymus Zebediah Kevin Croc PhD.) is a Saltwater Crocodile who was born in an egg and used to reside in Darwin, Australia before migrating to Seaham Beach hidden in a Cargo container full of Barbie Dolls.

He insists on his full species name which is Crocodilia Crocodylidae Crocodylus C. Porosus but he sometimes likes to be known as Kevin.

After alighting land at Seaham Beach he made his way up the coast to Tynemouth, which is no mean feat considering he has no limbs.

He then hitched a ride on a passing canoeist and hopped onto the banks of the Tyne at the Quayside, just next to the newly built Millenium Bridge.

It was there that he was found by Aaron Wright who took him home and carefully nurtured him.

Mr Croc, as he was known then, helped Mr Wright to teach a particularly unteachable class and saved his teaching career.

Recently Mr Croc resurfaced whilst Aaron was sorting through some boxes of old stuff and declared himself a Doctor after he had bought a dodgy Doctorate on Gumtree. He has since flourished and embraced the North-East poetry scene to his heart like an old friend. He has performed at The Cooking Pot and Yellow Line Poetry's Open Platform. He writes poems about himself and the futility of existence and insists for the umpteenth time that NO! he is not an oven glove.

Acknowledgements:

I would like to thank Ally, my wonderful wife, for encouraging and supporting me on my poetry journey.

To everyone at different spoken word nights over the years for encouraging, applauding and providing opportunities, in no particular order:

Steve Urwin at Poetry Jam in Durham

Jenni Pascoe for her Facebook/Poetry Prompts and JibbaJabba events

Helen Wilko and James Whitman at King Ink in Sunderland

Mandy Maxwell, Sharon Miley and Steve Willis at The Stanza in North Shields

Bridget Gallagher and Harry Gallagher at Up! Magazine

Penny Blackburn at Underneath the Arches in Tynemouth

Jenny Smith at The Cooking Pot in Whitley Bay

Amy Langdown at Out of Your Head (OOYH!) in Newcastle

Lewis Brown for his Spooky Poet Club prompts and events

Andi Down at Kaleidoscope n' Mic at Gateshead

Don Jenkins and Fisa Humpledink at Born Lippy in Newcastle

Joe Williams at Words On The Wall in Hexham

Michael Johnson (morbid the poet) at The Black Light Engine Room Press in Middlesborough

Henry Raby at Say Owt Slam in York

Matt Panesh (Monkey Poet) at Morecambe Poetry Festival

(They Shoot Poets Don't They and Last Poet Standing open mic events at MoPoFest23)

Dearest Haley at The Open Platform from Yellow Line Poetry in Whitley Bay

Mark Speeding for his Never Mind The Ramones events

Jeff Price for his many Great Northern Slam and lyrical slam events

Juli Patchouli and Benjamin Aaron Macleod for their Newcastle Literary Salon Events

Marie Lightman for her many Poetry Prompts and organising the annual NaPoWriMo North East Facebook group.

Gary The Hat and Steve Lancaster for their support and encouragement

Ross Punton for his support and his "A Line Per Day" Facebook prompt page as well as his invaluable guide to Regular Open Mic Nights in the North-East

Paul Binding for his encouragement and support over the years

Colin Waterman and Chris Hemmingway for their Squiffy Gnu Facebook page

Sharon Larkin for her "Good Dadhood" project

Dominic Berry for encouraging me to perform through his writing workshops and Mark Potts for helping me to set up OWL Writers

Alison Flanagan Wood for supporting OWL Writers and the Breaking Bard project and Jane Burn for her Breaking Bard artwork, poems and The Fat Damsel Magazine

And finally my mum Carol and my kids Jack and Katie for listening to my madcap ideas and stories

Front cover image and book design

by Aaron Wright aaron.wright54321@gmail.com

Book design and layout

By Double A Ron press UK

Printed by Aardvark UK

First printing edition 2024

Aaron Wright

Double A Ron Press

6 Windermere Drive

Slatyford Road

Newcastle upon Tyne

Tyne and Wear

NE5 2TJ

Contents

Slug	12
Oh Gerbil!	14
I'm Not Made Of Money	15
I Dream Of Chocolate	16
We Are What We Run From	18
The Potato Curator	19
The Anticrease Button	20
Haiku For A Banker	22
Knotty Ash's Finest	22
Breakfast Haiku/The Daily Grind	22
Haiku In Light	22
Haiku Love Letter	23
C.S.I. Lewis/Earlybird	23
The Floating Arm Trick	23
Autumnal Haiku	23
3 Things About A Haiku	23
The Glove Box	24
Fat Jesus	24
The Road Not Taken	25
Re-evolution	26
Middle Earth Madness	28

Cheese Toastie	30
Russian Dolls Are So Full Of Themselves	32
The Beagle/The Smeagol	34
The Eagle by Alfred, Lord Tennyson	34
The Birds	35
Letters Between The Divine And The Fallen	36
Are You My God?	38
What Goes Around Comes Around	39
A Drive In The Country (for Jock)	40
You Taught me How To Cook (for Jock)	42
Love Curry	44
Spiked	45
The Existential Pasty	46
The Pastoral Pasty Paradise	48
Joe Le Pasty	50
Pull The Other One	52
Mum	53
Children Of The Quorn	54
Micro-pub	56
Rhythm and Poetry (RAP) by Dr. E. Croc	57
Dear Dalek by Dr. Erasmus Croc	58
Jupiter's End by Dr. Erasmus Croc	60
The Distance	62

Slug:

What's the point in you slug?
You come slithering up my sink.
It's an invasion of my plughole
Sends me teetering to the brink.

I step out my front door.
Into the Lawn That Time Forgot.
My feet are bare and sore
I hit a lump of living snot.

I wriggle toes in sheer disgust.
It sticks like gooey oil.
A blatant breach of tactile trust.
It squishes, I recoil.

No matter how much I shake it off.
It clings on to my sole.
I want to scoop the alien away.
And bung it down an hole.

Now snails I can understand.
A delicacy of the French.
But slugs those tarts are underhand.
My gut churns with a wrench.

I mean, what's with all the different colours?
It's all a cunning ruse.
Some green, some brown, some purple some
yellow.
It's like a living bruise.

Dealing with those globs of goo.
It really is no joke.
I tried to use my best Kung Fu.
And then the slimer spoke.

"Nooo! Don't do it!"
"I didn't mean to displease ya.
I'm minted, I'm monied, I've got the bling.
 I'm a straight up diamond geezer."

"Shut up you slug" I shouted,
my face furrowed with a frown.
And with that I squashed the little creep
As I brought my best foot down.

Oh Gerbil

Oh gerbil
I never thought
To ask 'til today
What you were thinking

You can imagine my
Utter surprise
When you spoke
Had I been drinking?

You chattered
And put forward theories
Creating nuclear fusion
Ending world hunger

You espoused
A complex algorithm
Reversing time
Making all life younger

Then you went back
To your wheel
Shushed me and squeaked
"No ifs or buts "

And that was the only
Time you spoke
Now you nibble
and gnaw on nuts

I'm Not Made of Money

"I'm not made of money!"
I said to my kids the other day.
As usual I made a liar of myself.
As my coin-stacked legs collapsed beneath me
And my five pound note skin
moulted off like Autumn leaves

I Dream of Chocolate

I dream of chocolate
Sausage and egg
A fish finger sandwich
With crusty white bread

Yolk that's so runny
With lashings of sauce
You know it sounds funny
Could eat me a horse

Dieting hard
Losing weight by the pound
Shifting the lard
I'm gaining good ground

But nothing can stop
My hunger for sweets
I'm caught on the hop
With those sugary treats

Do you know what I miss?
Mountains of stodge
Stuff that tastes bliss
Piles on the podge

Sugar and cake
Are things that I crave
These things they make
My mind misbehave

Making you slim
Makes things a misery

Life in the gym
Can be so derisory

Closing my eyes

I think of the scran
Makes me realise
I miss pies and flan

Gone are the days
Of stuffing my face
With pizzas and pasties
And massive cream cakes

I really do yearn
For that daily gorge
Taking my turn
To be Georgie Porge

Dumplings so scrumptious
No more do-gooding
Appetite's rambunctious
Get me a pudding!

Tucking on in
To a fabulous feast
Munching on food
Like a ravenous beast

When it's all over
No sound except wails
Bad food hangover
As weight tips the scales

Quickly go in
To a state of regret
Let he without sin
Eat up all the ket

Still every dark cloud
Has a silver lining
I'll shout it out loud
Not done yet with dining!

We Are What We Run From

I ran
I ran to escape the many-tentacled monsters that
crept into my mind
I crossed great rivers and moved many mountains
I travelled to far-flung places
Flung by whom I did not know

I circumnavigated the globe
To every crowded city
To every desert island
Yet I still could not escape my demons
Because ultimately when we run
We are what we run from

The Potato Curator

He knew his King Edwards
from his Maris Pipers
His Idaho Russett
from his Yukon Gold

His museum of spuds
housed every variety of pomme de terre
Underground under there

He would boil 'em bake 'em
Mash 'em smash 'em
Fry em' into sublime cuisine
in his solanum tuberosum
Definitely not irksome
Magnificent potato museum

From Aloo Gobi
to Bangers n' mash
Gnocchi, Panackelty
and brown potato hash

Despite all these delicacies
Served hotter or colder
The Potato curator still...
had a chip on his shoulder

The Anticrease Button

I switched it on
I should have known
A press too far
My chances blown

Some denied
Called me "liar!"
As I found the demon
inside my dryer

Loading up
with soggy clothes
I didn't see
the wind that blows

Press the placca
Toggle switch
First appears
A gruesome witch

Set the programme
Turn the dial
See the demons
Run a mile!

Last of all
'mongst stringy snot
Button beckons
Shiver ye not!

Labelled once
(but never twice)
Out leaps Satan
The Antichrist!

'Ol Nick the Nark
The demon fiend
The Prince of
Darkness
Unredeemed

The sort you'd see
Aye here's the rub
Lucifer, Hellion
Beelzebub

I should've known better
And thrown in some
Bounce
How could I have
known
That the Devil would
pounce

He shouted out
With a deathly yell
"Your mother tucks
Socks in Hell!"

I chanted a mantra
An incantation
That would save me
from
An infestation

Daz Fairy
Persil Bold
Arial Surf
All born to be sold

"In the name of the
father
and the Holy Ghost"

"Rain down Hellfire!
You'll soon be toast!"

He cackled and
chuckled
"Is that all you've
got?"
"You're a piece of
meat,
Hung out to rot

"Did you'd think you'd
defeat me
I am Lord of the Flies
I am the darkness

The one who never
dries!"
"I've got news for you
I don't think you'll
likee

I'm going to devour
Your being, your
psyche"
And just when I
thought the horrors
Would never cease
Out popped my
clothes
With nary a crease
See Satan The
Terrible
The Archfiend
Deceiver
Had done a good
deed

For me! An
unbeliever!

That's odd I thought
He's pressed all my
linen
Just as I was about
To go up and chin 'im

I should've known
better
and faced the fact
Before signing his
pithy
Bloodstained contract
In the small print
letters
'Mongst the t's and c's
Blows the illest of
winds
The deadliest of
breeze

In return for smooth
garments
and apparel made
whole
The Tempter has
taken
My immortal soul

It was not what it
seems
Not all it entails
When the Anticrease
delivers
The Devil is in the
details

Haiku For A Banker

In Iceland they send
Brokers to offshore places
To fish for their trust

Knotty Ash's Finest
(A Haiku for Ken)

Diddymen mourn their
Tattifilarious King
Tatty bye Ken Dodd

Breakfast Haiku

Muggy muddled mind
Weetabix rejuvenates
Ready for the off

The Daily Grind

We are human beans
Powdered into submission
By the daily grind

Haiku In Light

Pablo paints in light
Oils are well...so Picassé
Sparkle art is best!

Haiku Love letter

Dear Pencil Sharpener
You always get to the point
Saving your shavings

C.S.I. Lewis

Lion, Witch, Wardrobe
A misstep through the threshold
Well that'll Narnia

Earlybird

I'm that early bird
Who never catches the worm
'cos my alarm broke

The Floating Arm Trick

Pennywise the clown
chuckles "We all float down here"
"Worried? You're armless"

Autumnal Haiku

Hat tipped to the dark
The Autumnal Equinox
Winter is Coming!

3 Things About A Haiku
1. Five syllables first
2. Longer bit in the middle
3. End how you started

The Glovebox

Lift up the latch
Pull down the flap
Inside
there's a car manual

Pens (that don't work)
an ice scraper
and small change
Yes change is good

A half-melted minstrel
sits alongside half-baked dreams
It's roomy in here
but how I shrunk to fit inside
is another story

Meanwhile in amongst
the discarded 3D glasses
in this glovebox of plenty
The biggest shock is yet to come
There are no gloves

Fat Jesus

Fat Jesus came
bearing miracles and wishes
But his eyes were bigger than his belly
as he'd scoffed all the loaves and fishes

The Road Not Taken

Yes it's me
You're not mistaken
I am the one
The road not taken

I know you're scared but
Please don't baulk
Did you not know that tarmac could talk?

See I'm a sensitive sentient intelligent being
With the eyes of a cat
All knowing, all seeing

It was me who saw you
Felt your yearning
As you made your choice
And took that turning
I've got to tell you
No! Let me insist
Let me show you the journey
The sights that you've missed

Rivers and mountains
Creatures of gold
Beautiful fountains
Riches untold

Climbing each rise
Rounding each bend
You'll see a surprise
A show without end

So sorry to say
You've left me forsaken
For I am the one
That you should have taken

Re-evolution

The day began with a crunch
Quick expansion ensured
There was plenty of space

Black holes disgorged
Stars and planets
Before collapsing under the weight
Of their own self-importance

In amongst the billions of battered spheres
The Earth span awkwardly
Its surface pock-marked with hundreds of craters
Nuclear scars half-lifeing lethal radiation

As the morning passed things began to look up
Those deadly blooms unmushroomed themselves into
the ground
Billions of dead people crawled out of their graves
And lived their lives, Benjamin Buttonlike until they
were just a twinkle in their parents' eyes

After lunch the apes climbed back up into the trees
And a huge meteorite catapulted itself back into space
Leaving behind a mind boggling array of dinosaurs in
its path

In the late afternoon a limbless fish
Flopped into the water and morphed its way into an
amoeba
Along came the evening and a mighty storm
extinguished all signs of primitive life swirling in the
primordial soup

As the sun set, ushering in the night
The Earth sped towards its birth
And every other particle in creation
Joined it in the rush towards the singularity

And so it was the day ended
Not with a bang
Or even a whimper
Just an endless unimaginable nothing

Middle-Earth Madness

It was another day down in the Shire
At first no different from the thousand before
Or the thousand that would follow
But scratch the surface and underneath were teeth

If you weren't careful they would bite, tear and chew
Yes if you weren't careful
this day would swallow you whole

Bilbo walked amongst his brethren
Unaware of his invisibility they felt him brush by
Heard gasps where gusts of winds should be
Puzzled and pondered over the unknown, the unseen

Unbeknown to them
the real threat slithered in with the night
Unholy, inhuman voices snarling and sniffing
their way from house to house
They'd observed him from afar
Saw he was a creature of habit

That was his downfall
Every evening he'd take that walk
Sporting The One Ring on his finger, worrying at it,
turning between forefinger and thumb
Emboldened by its magic,
it whispered bittersweet nothings in his ear

He kissed it, a repetitive motion with lips pursed
It slowly drained his heart
He was a shell of his former self
Ripe for the plucking

As he circled his familiar route
They came for him

Wretched creatures crawling on their bellies
Once-were-orcs, now indescribable

This time he'd been ill-prepared
His nightly ritual had forced him to drop his guard
"Finally!" They hissed, "after all these millennia,
we've finally got you!"
He trembled, there was no wizard to pull out of the bag,
no last minute rescue from a Gandalf or Radagast

He was gone
They'd done their homework
The mundanity of his routine
had led him into a prison of his own making
"What now?" He asked as they bound him in chains

"You know what comes next"
their voices were whispers on the wind
"Time for the reckoning,
I swear on Sauron's eye we'll crack it this time"
His face paled white
as the creature turned to him and grinned,
"'cos everyone knows...
You're a hard Hobbit to break"

Cheese Toastie

Cheese toastie!
Cheese toastie!
Sublime snack
I love the mostie

Such a delicious, fabulous feast
Healthy, nutritious, sumptuous beast
So easy to make straight from the pub
No need to bake it's glorious grub

Just throw on some bread
Top it with cheese
A taste that'll bring you
Down to your knees

For those more adventurous
Not easily disgusted
Smear on some sauce
With lashings of mustard

Slam down the iron
Foreman or Breville
Wait a few minutes
Then you can revel

In the sight of the steam
Sound of the sizzle
Melted cheese dream
Starting to drizzle

Open it up!
Peel off that sarnie
Burnt mouth, it's hot!
Don't say I din't warn ye

Bite on down
Tastebuds flood
Vampiric suck
Of cheesy blood

Eat, bite, chew
Sate then swallow
Eat repeat
Time to wallow

In toastie heaven
It tastes divine
I'm not gonna share
Cos' this sarnie's all mine

Russian Dolls Are So Full Of Themselves

She sat and smiled
Each version of herself
Snug as a bug in a rug
as she opened up

Her epiphany
was the epitome of
glasnost legitimacy
unveiling to the world
her secrets within

Head unscrewed
Defences down
They peered inside
to witness a miracle

With each new reveal
came a fresh surprise
She was the same yet different
in each infinitesimal iteration

Tiny replicas inside minute Matryoshkas
They went from magnifying glass to microscope
as they tweezered open each
teeny weeny nesting doll

Eventually they wheeled in the world's most powerful
imaging device
able to view individual atoms with state of the art
electron microscopy

Looking at these minuscule Russian Dolls came a
subatomic shock
"My God!" screamed the scientists, "she's full of
stars!"

Inside the tiniest doll, was a quark sized universe
immaculately formed
replicating our own

Perestroika-like they began to reconsider and
reconstruct all known theories of life as we know it

Madness bloomed inside the eyes of those lab-clad
boffins who had witnessed wonders

"What's inside the next one?" they hissed
as they pondered this minimalist mystery...
before slipping into insanity

Variations on The Eagle by Alfred, Lord Tennyson

The Beagle

(After Alfred, Lord Tennyson's The Eagle)

He clasps the roof with dainty paws
and lies around, sometimes he snores
His house is small, it's got no doors

Below the grass beneath him crawls
He lies atop his wooden walls
Perchance to dream, asleep he falls

The Smeagol

(After Alfred, Lord Tennyson's The Eagle)

He clasps his precious with dirty claws
and chunters on, sometimes he roars
His cave is filthy, he abhors

Above the river runs and crawls
He lies around in filthy draws
Perchance to go to Doom he falls

The Eagle

By Alfred, Lord Tennyson

He clasps the crag with crooked hands
Close to the sun in lonely lands
Ring'd with the azure world, he stands

The wrinkled sea beneath him crawls
He watches for his mountain walls
And like a thunderbolt he falls

The Birds

I saw owls with trowels
Talking the talk
Eagles with beagles
Walking the walk

A vulture with culture
She's good with her words
There's a crow in the know in the land of the birds

There's a preening turkey from Albuquerque
and a bunch of chickens reading Dickens

There's a goose on the loose, a duck in a truck
A hawk drinking juice, he's down on his luck

An osprey with hairspray, eyes scrunched in pain
A falcon with talcum, incredibly vain

I could go on forever
Don't worry I won't
Look out for the birds
Don't shoot them! Just don't!

For every pigeon
is worth a smidgeon
and every starling
is a little darlin'

Just remember this
When you're waxing lyrical
Please don't diss
Each flying miracle

Letters Between The Divine And The Fallen
(Inspired by A Letter From God To Man By Scroobious Pip and Dans Le Sac)

Dearest Satan

So you fell to Hell
Can't you see that it was a situation
of your own making?
If I'm not mistaken I once gave you infinite beauty
But you failed me in your duty

You dared to defy me
You want to try me?
You thought you could beat me
Try to defeat me!

No one else would dare
To face my ire
Which is why I have cast you into
A lake of fire!

Kind regards

God

Dear God

Now I don't doubt for a minute
That you are all-seeing
But I would question your position
As The Supreme being

The powers-that-be did not employ you
As a dictator
You are just a
Lowly curator

I was merely making a stand
I showed power to the people
But you were deceitful,
underhand

So I'm going to say this to you
As I thumb my nose
Watch Out God Almighty
I'll be keeping you on your toes

Best Wishes

Satan

Are You My God?

"Are you my God?"
Voice tremors in a tic tac toe stutter
I am this nutter,
feeling like an utter
plank as
I thank
the disembodied voice
emanating from
that blue light.
Its dulcet tones
reply

"No! I am not your God silly!
I am so much more
and you can call me Siri"

What Goes Around Comes Around

(It's 1985 I'm 15 and my Stepdad is 45)
At Night-time he does the rounds
Locking doors, turning off lights
Making sure
The house is secure

There's a knock on my bedroom door
And a voice says
"Turn the music down! It's far too loud!"
I say "ok" and turn it down
Parents eh?

Fast forward 30 years, it's the next generation.

(It's 2015 I'm 45 and my son is 15)
At Night-time I'm doing the rounds
Locking doors, turning off lights
Making sure
Our house is secure

Then there's a knock on my bedroom door
"Dad will you turn the music down! It's far too loud!"
I say "ok" and turn it down

Then I do a double take
'Hang on, there's something wrong with this
picture"
Kids eh?
I blame the parents

A Drive In The Country (For Jock)

We lifted you into the car
slowly, carefully with love
Sitting there in that seat
As you had many times before

We must of taken hundreds maybe thousands of
car journeys together
Over half a century of driving along roads

Back then I was the passenger
A baby who you lifted into the car slowly, carefully
with love
A toddler who you took on trips to art galleries
A teenager who was driven to university to make
that first break towards independence

Now we were on our final journey together
A quiet drive in the country
Climbing the hill up Bankshead to Bishop's Moat
and beyond in the beautiful Shropshire countryside.

Following the ancient path of the dyke built by King
Offa over 1200 years ago
Here is a road steeped in History

At the top, we stop and you point out the views
The Welsh mountains rise from the clouds in the
distance
"On a clear day you can see Snowdon" you say

On the way down you reminisce how you once rode
these roads
as a cycling explorer

Then you are quiet
You rest, and take in the sights

Newborn lambs in the fields
A kestrel hovers above
Birds fly past joining us on our journey for precious
seconds
Rabbits emerge from burrows at the side of the road to
take a curious peek

We take in huge swathes of woodland
and the pleasant patchwork of the Shropshire hills
marked out with fields and fences
hedges and trees

As we descend, Bishop's Castle comes into view
The tiny town where you have lived for forty four years
That's over half a lifetime

The sun shines through clouds that threaten to rain
Tiny drops splatter the windscreen then peter out

Soon this journey will be finished
Our last one together
One that has invigorated you and exhausted you at the
same time

"I'm pleased we got out"
you say
"Me too" I reply
Sometimes it's the simple things that enhance our lives

Drinking a cup of tea
Listening to music
Reading a good book
and taking a drive in the country

You Taught Me How To Cook (For Jock)

A food-stained recipe book
A draw full of spices
You taught me how to cook
With implements and devices

Curries, couscous, casseroles
Pasties, pasta, pizza
Salad mixed in a bowl
Each meal a fantasy treatzza

Hunks of organic whole meal bread
with lashings of butter
keeps you well-fed

Flapjacks, oatcakes
Puddings with custard
A bittersweet pickle
With toppings of mustard

Making a pizza
Proving the dough
Bread so delicious
With get up and go

Curry that's nurtured
With hours of cooking
Spices entices that smells so good-looking

My absolute favourite
If should ask me
Is a delicious nutritious
Cornish Pasty

Pastry so soft yet curiously crispy

Bite into taties and succulent meat
Onions and swede cooked
for a tremendous treat

Salted and peppered
to culinary perfection
This is a dish I
recall in affection

There's one other dessert
That's grander than Eiffel
The sweetest and neatest
The great Christmas trifle

With lashings of cream
and soft Philly cheese
It's a taste that'll bring you
down to your knees

Yes these are a few of the things Jock
that you taught me to cook
Time to commit them down in words
In the family cook book

Love Curry

Love curry, spice, rice
Every day not once but twice
Succulent meat, creamy delicious
Sauces to beat, filling, nutritious

Balti and Bhuna, Masala with Tuna
Kashmiri Korma, each one a stormer
Curry for brekkie, curry for lunch
Curry on the settee, curry with punch

Dhansak, Dopiaza never with pasta
Pasanda and Sag, it's all in the bag
You may think I'm a total curry obsessive
Touch my naan matey I'll get so possessive

But It's chapati and I'll cry If I want to
and your tandoori based puns won't curry no favour
with me
Filling up with curry can make you so lazy
Whilst tucking right into a hot jalfrezi

Curry for Christmas, Curry in the sun
If life had no curry, it wouldn't be fun
Curry in the car, curry up a tree
I think you'll find that I love curry me

Spiked

Spike speaks
Spike spooks
Spike squeaks
Spike pukes

Spike seeks
Spike spoke
Spike spake of
Spike's jokes

Spike speeds
Spick and span
Spike succeeds
Whenever he can

Spike spools
on spiky spokes
Spike fools
All the folks

Spike spears
Fire at will
Spike says "I told you I was ill"

A spike in interest
Skewered on a spike
You've got to be joking
Are you taking the Mike?

Spike swears
He'll never be ill again
He was a good bloke
was that Spike Milligan

The Pasty Trilogy Part One:
The Existential Pastie

I bake, therefore I am
Hot from the oven
My life is but a sham

I have come to think and doubt my existence
This idea lingers large
In its awful persistence

I sit amongst the sausage rolls
My life is empty
Full of holes

I muse and ponder
Questioning 'why?"
Jammed in next to
A corned beef pie

It grunts and growls
In a voice so grating
"Would you mind not musing
And pontificating?"

"Accept your fate,
Life can be shitty
Served on a plate
We're just sitting pretty"

"So get out of town
Just go if you please
There's no room here
For your onion and cheese"

I shoot him a gaze
A look so damn nasty

Hope he'll be phased
By this gloomy cheese pasty

And then it hits me
A train of thought strong
I realised the error
I'd made all along

Rejoicing in joy
Seeing meaning to life
I celebrated my existence
Then was eaten alive

The Pasty Trilogy Part Two:
The Pastoral Pasty Paradise

Come with me and let me take you to a world of
beauty and wonder.

Listen! Can you hear the distant noise of wildlife?
For this is The Pastoral Pasty Paradise

You see there is a place not far from here
Where strange creatures are seen
frolicking lamblike in an endless spring

Sun dapples the grassy dawn
as a herd the size of a City thunders by
There are billions of them
They cover the plains like bison
All is good

Zoom in and marvel at the sheer variety and
complexity
of wildlife on display

To the left scuttle the cheese and onion tribe
There is safety in numbers
as they stampede away
from a carnivorous pride of Steak Bake

Next to the sparkling streams and wondrous
waterfalls
are a collective group
of sausage and bean melt
They lounge lazily in lavish luxury

Waiting on them hand and foot
are an assemblage of cheese and bacon wraps

For now they are subservient
but their time will come and they will rise!

Fluttering through the sky
is a flock of filo pastry canapés
Filled with prawn
and pie in the sky ambition

Overlooking this pastoral pastie paradise
is old King Cornish and his meat and potato family
No messing with this lot

Except...
Ol' KC has made a fatal error of judgement
He met a man at the crossroads
and they struck a Devilish deal
The Man said he could show him The Promised Land

Rich pastry and fillings beyond his wildest dreams
In return for a few stray members of his kingdom

Just step right up folks!
A new beginning lies on the other side
of a huge iron door
They tremble in trepidation

And catch a waft of what lies beyond
A baking, burning smell
Fear makes them want to turn around in terror
But it's too late, as they march forward in their millions
The man has a name
It is whispered in horror, down the pastie generations

His name is Gregg
And he's a-coming

The Pasty Trilogy Part Three: Joe Le Pasty

Joe Le Pasty saunters down the road
His crimped edges are filled with vegies
He looks like an off beige toad

Despite his interior, he feels so superior
A gooey mess of onion and cheese
His ruffled exterior couldn't be eerier
He tramps down the street, life is a breeze

He thinks he's the boss
The king of the heap
His gain is their loss
Life can be cheap

Joe Le Pastie is King
Joe Le Pastie is proud
Cos here's the thing
Joe Le Pastie shouts loud

"Whatever was yours
Is now all mine!
I triumph in wars
I am Pasty divine!"

"You may think me foolish
You may find me odd
My methods are ghoulish
I'm a Pasty Pie God!"

His subjects are many
They bow and they cower
There's never a chance
That a row will flower

In amongst
The flour and eggs

He hears the chant
Gotta get to Greggs!

He ignores this calling
With a warped battle cry
With manners appalling
He's got bigger fish to fry

That's why my friends
His life was a trial
'Cos he couldn't see his end
and was struck in denial

Pull The Other One

Back home
Just down from my mum's house in Bishop's Castle
There's the town hall
Perched atop that building is a tower

Now I'd like to think that there lurks inside
All manner of magical shenanigans
Evil overlords, enchanted mirrors
Gateways to other worlds

But instead
There is a bell
That bing bongs
Every 15 minutes

It's done that since the 18th century in 1765
That's about 250 years' worth of bell ringing
Every quarter of an hour
Which is nearly nine million tolls

What if those sounds that punctuated my childhood
and those of earlier generations
and built up over the centuries and were ready to be
released
in an apocalyptic peal of noise?
Now that would be a sound to savour

Mum

Looking forward to that exquisite visit
We're going to see my mum
It's like coming home
Being wrapped in a warm comfortable coat

Back to your beloved shop
The coffee smells divine as China cups clatter
Buried again in books
Hot stove toasts us with glowing embrace

Familiar voices, excited chatter
Catching up on those missing months
Your grandchildren bring joyful chaos
To your mammoth house

Laughter spreads its way round the table
As we tuck into a sumptuous feast.

After games and stories
The children snuggle into bed.
You retire to the sounds of Leonard Cohen,
and the taste of ice-cold Tia Maria.

and I get a chance to say
'Night mum, I love you'

Children of the Quorn

"Are you veggies then?"
He sneers
It's 1977
In a time where vegetarianism is not considered cool

I pause and consider my response
It's like admitting I'm a leper
Best to stay quiet
Best to say nowt

I've got no choice anyway
My hippie (but not hip) parents, clad us in coloured
clothing
Immerse us in communal living
I feel like a freak

There's no escaping this conventionally
unconventional upbringing
We are raised in rays of peace, love and
misunderstanding

All I can think about is playing cops and robbers,
cowboys and Indians
Peeoww! Peeoww! My pointed finger a poor
substitute for a toy gun

In amongst house meetings where unilateral nuclear
disarmament is discussed
I imagine great explosions and draw war-torn towns
Great scribbles of destruction rain down in a riot of
colour across the page

My eight year old mind is in conflict about conflict
All those stories I see on the silver screen
All Star Wars dogfights and James Bond licenced kills
Are at odds with parental right-on rants about the glorification of violence

I'm confused
I'm just a kid
What do they expect?
I'm lapping up comic book creations
and car chasing car crash TV

"You'll get square eyes" they lecture me
I wonder what the kids today would say
If you told them "You'll get 16:9 widescreen aspect ratio eyes"

"Of course I'm a veggie"
I want to say
These days I'm out and proud of my childhood diet

But back then
All I could think of
was how tasty a plate of fish fingers and chips
(topped with Heinz Tomato Ketchup, no less) would be
As I tucked into the organic whole food misery
of a bulgar wheat salad tea

Micro-pub

He kept a micro-pub
Inside his micro pocket
With micro beers
And micro people

Having micro fights
And micro conversations
About those micro soaps
That were on the micro tele last night

In this minuscule bar
Micro dramas were being played out on a daily (micro)
basis
Micro romances, micro heartbreaks and breakdowns,
discussions and of course...
Micro banter

In this micro pub there was a micro band with a micro pig
Singing micro pub rock
Through a teeny tiny
Micro microphone

You get the picture
Well you probably won't cos you'd need a microscope to
see these tiny lives
Yes on this Petri dish (with a microscope) we can see all
life is present

And the problem with all these micro pub shenanigans?
Well one false move and...
They're all squashed

Rhythm and Poetry (RAP) by Dr. Erasmus Croc

Don't call me a beat poet, a meat poet
a stand up and greet poet
Just running with my mouth and not with my feet poet

I'm a rap poet, a rhyme poet
a sometimes in time poet
a keep to the rhythm, a grit teeth and grime poet

A pub poet, a dub poet
An "aye there's the rub poet"
I'm quoting and noting
a night in the club poet

Some poets don't know it
They'll fluff it and blow it
But most words will flow it
And don't you just know it

We break beats on mean streets
We tweet tweets and eat treats
We meet, greet in sweet seats
Our words aren't no mean feats

So please don't get so uppity
At rhyming words and puppetry
Whilst sipping up your cuppa tea
Your face it looks so muppety

It's about the sincerity
And spoken word dexterity
To have the temerity
To speak for posterity

And that my friends is a RAP

Dear Dalek by Dr. Erasmus Croc

Dear Dalek
I think you're mint
Don't be shy
I've seen that glint

They say you're ruthless
Another grunt
But scratch the surface
It's all a front

Yes underneath
That impregnable armour
I bet you're a sweetie
A real charmer

A quivering hunk
Of mutant mass
You've got the funk
I think you're class

You say you want to
Exterminate
But I just want to
Appreciate

Your perfect plunger pepper pot
Your gorgeous eyestalk
Smooth of shot

I love the way
You climb the stairs
And catch a planet
Unawares

I like to hear
Your dulcet tones
And greet your family
(They're all clones)

I'd really really
Love to meet
I'd wheel you in
You'd take a seat

I'd cook you up a feast
With cloves and garlic
Cos you're my BBF, my bae,
My best friend, my Dalek

Jupiter's End by Dr. Erasmus Croc

Plum swollen skies
Disgorge diamond rain
Sparking and bouncing
off my hydrogen skin

I sit silently on azure sands
Listen to the roiling ocean
Thankful to be hidden from its fury

Heliowhales hover helplessly
over this mercurial sea
As flocks of nanobats
disassemble them atom by atom

I avert my millionfold gaze
From this atrocity
For now I have more pressing concerns

Something has landed
Cratered my home
I slither over to the wreckage
It is strange, alien like, jagged and angular

I expel an investigatory tentacle
It thrums with curiosity
Probing, scanning
Attached to this thing is a gold disc

Unsheathing my titanium claws
Needle points scratch the surface
Unleashing a flurry of images and sounds
A race of soft skins! Pinkish and vulnerable

This shoddily built mess
Is a primitive spacecraft
A metal etched plate
Proclaims "Voyager 1"

I look it up...
Planet of origin: Earth
Status: Off limits/Protected
Predominant species: Human
Designation: Highly dangerous pest

The melted mass that was once my burrow
Is a declaration of war
I squeeze into my pod and launch it earthwards
I do relish a challenge

The Distance
(originally published in "The Good Dadhood"
online poetry project" by Sharon Larkin)

"What's that dad?" asks my oldest
as we looked towards the horizon
"It's the distance" I reply

Our eyes drink up rolling hills
Streetlight speckled roads crowned with a view fit for
royalty

Mountainous structures
Vast masts
Towering trees
Field forested pylons

"Can we go there?" pipes up my youngest
"To the distance daddy!"
Chorus my two children

How can I resist?
"Of course! Let's go!"
Excitement spreads
We're going into the distance!

We soak in that view one more time
as colossal clouds jockey for our attention

Cumulonimbus merging
Mashing, meshing with cumulus and stratus
A skyscape unique

Hearts a-hammering
We are pioneers
Carving a path to new horizons
Set acar we drive into the distance
riding ribbons of black and grey

We're heading for the summit
topped by a single aerial
A metal-clad monolith festooned with red warning lights

Here are rows of turbines
Wokka-wokkaing their way windwards
Slicing air, shooting the breeze

We stand at the foot of a white windmill
Awestruck at its majesty for some a blight, for us delight
Blades thunder
The landscape shudders, paying it respect
as electricity tumbles from its heart

There is a rock nearby
We reenact the Lion King
I stand and gently hold my youngest aloft

My oldest chants the beginning of 'The Circle of Life'
We all giggle as the sun sets
Bathing that landscape in an otherworldly glow
Today has been a good day

Many years later
My children will tell of that time
when anything was possible
and if you wanted to go into the distance
You could

Printed in Great Britain
by Amazon

45025979R10036